SCIENCE ACTIVITIES
for Christian Children

SCIENCE ACTIVITIES
for Christian Children

Process Skills Development

Revised

Clifton Keller, Ph.D.

and Jeanette Appel, B.A.

International Standard Book Number: 0-930192-15-X

Printed by Mountain Missionary Press,
P.O. Box 279, Harrisville, N.H. 03450, U.S.A.

GAZELLE PUBLICATIONS
5580 Stanley Drive
Auburn, CA 95603

CONTENTS

Predicting

Introduction

From the publisher

Welcome to the thoroughly revised edition of *Science Activities for Christian Children.* Two experiments have been added at the suggestion of my father and many have been expanded.

We would appreciate your comments and recommendations for future editions. What would you like to see added? Which activities might be improved, and how?

May the Author of science be your Guide and your children's Friend.

Ted Wade, Jr.

General tips

Interesting lessons, ones that make lasting impressions, require planning. As a teacher, your preparation should include clear notes about what you expect to happen, assembly of the needed materials, and actual working through your demonstrations or the student activities.

You should hesitate to offer help unless dangerous chemicals or other hazards are present.

Demonstrations allow more explanation and usually teach more quickly. On the other hand, student activities or experiments provide handling practice and teach, too. Demonstrations should be orderly and presented in such a way that each step is clearly visible to all students. Preparing chalkboard illustrations or posters to point out important aspects of current activities helps students be aware of salient facts. The presence of a beaker containing colored water is certain to elicit interest and questions.

The following organization has been useful in schools lacking equipment, space, or both. The class is divided into groups of two. Each pair is assigned to a station, and each station is planned for a different activity. The science period for one or two days is used for setup, experimenting and making the pair the "authorities" for their activity. The students are required to prepare a lesson sheet for their experiment that includes rewriting the teacher's directions. They also make up question sheets to test the other students' understanding of the experiment. The authorities are responsible for replacing materials used or equipment broken, for reorganizing the set each day after use, and for grading the other students' responses to the question sheet.

When the authorities are prepared, a rotation procedure begins in which one member of the pair advances to a new experiment to become the "student" and the other member remains behind to be the "teacher." The following day or time period, the students rotate once more with the original pairs again together but at a new station.

After the first rotation, the classroom teacher will talk only to the authorities about any particular experiment so that if the "teacher" of the day is unable to answer a question, he or she looks to the other authority. If that student does not know the answer, he asks the adult teacher and the answer is channeled back to the one that posed the question.

In some cases, the classroom teacher may not know the answer, and it becomes her or his responsibility to look it up or to ask someone else to design the necessary experiment for finding out.

Assigning the more difficult experiments to a slower student has an interesting effect. Answering other student's questions builds the self-image and brings the realization that others also need help at times. Repeating the same explanation several times firmly establishes the ideas in his or her own memory.

Maximum learning results when the same concept is developed in several different ways. For example, each station could deal with the topic, surface tension. (See the experiment in the section, "Using Numbers.") One lab station could view a filmstrip, another might make certain parts of a bulletin board, and a third could write a report about surface tension. The remaining stations might be assigned to study the topic emphasizing a different process skill.

The integration of spiritual lessons into the science program requires special planning. Extra care is needed to make certain the lessons are not just tacked on. These lessons will be less effective if they are overdone. It is important to look for "teachable moments" or to create them. Hopefully this guide will provide a perspective that will encourage teachers and parents to look for opportunities to combine faith and learning.

We would emphasize that the spiritual lessons are not something that students should memorize or learn for a later response on a test. If to a general question such as, "What did you learn from this experiment?" a student responds with a spiritual lesson, the teacher will have been successful! Teachers should remember that heart-to-heart comments such as "You know, boys and girls, sin is like that . . . isn't it?" are more effective than saying "The spiritual lesson for today is. . . ."

Teachers, parents and students should be encouraged to think of their own lessons. Often those written by someone else seem contrived or trivial, but to the originator, they are genuine insights into Christian living. The most effective spiritual lessons are those that call attention to a truth when the child re-encounters the phenomenon in day-to-day activities. For example, a class I taught measured a space on our campus equivalent in size to Noah's ark. Now I cannot pass the spot without thinking of the ark. After Christ told stories about the "lilies of the field," no doubt hearers recalled the lessons as they saw the lily on their way to work or while taking an evening stroll.

Learning process skills

Science has a dual nature—product and process. As product, it is the well-defined body of knowledge we usually think of as the facts of science. This includes a systematization of cause-and-effect relationships that begins with observations and leads to generalizations, to theories, and eventually to laws.

Science teaching at the elementary school level attempts to go beyond delivering factual information —the product aspect—and looks to learning that will transfer to meeting general life needs. Thus children learn the thinking skills used in acquiring new knowledge—the process of science.

The process skills are generally considered to be:

* Observing
* Measuring
* Distinguishing spatial
   and temporal relationships
* Classifying
* Communicating
* Using numbers
* Inferring
* Predicting
* Hypothesizing
* Controlling variables
* Analyzing
* Interpreting
* Defining operationally

For our presentation here, we have selected those skills most appropriate for children at what Piaget calls the preoperational and concrete-operational levels of intellectual development.

The process skills overlap. Activities on inferring or predicting incorporate the skills of observing, classifying, communicating, and so on. The actual category to which any of our experiments or activities belongs is clearly subject to interpretation by teachers as is the grade or age level and the degree of difficulty. For example, if the mathematics is too difficult, you might want to allow the students to use a calculator.

This activity set is organized according to seven process skills. Its purpose is to assist teachers and parents in using and developing science lessons that help students view science as a constantly expanding dynamic search for ways to benefit humankind. We feel this is best accomplished by a balanced approach including the spiritual dimension.

Each description attempts to provide all the necessary information to plan an activity that encourages children to interact with things, to develop their own ideas, and to ask questions.

Acknowledgments

The material presented here has been selected from a collection of over a thousand activity reports, and has been rewritten as needed for publication. Each activity description was chosen for a particular reason, be it the spiritual lesson, the experiment, or even a catchy title.

Special recognition is given to Joni Darmody, Shari Ware, Yolanda Drake, Pam Stimac, and Sharie Green. Other contributors include Saba Anderson, Ellen Baushke, Leon Brown, Cindy Carlsen, Jenny Erickson, Melanie Freeth, Pam Gustafson, Elwyn Hyde, Karen Johnston, Chloricia Lake, Cynthia Lake, C. Lawson, Phyllis Lee, Karen McLaren, Dewane More, Nanci Motschiedler, Joan Prouty, Carole Sannes, Linda Sherwin, Sandra Veldman, Vivienne Watts, and Everett Westmore.

Observing

Magnetic attraction

Objective: The student will develop skills in observation by watching how iron filings are attracted to magnets.

Spiritual lesson: The love of Jesus is so strong that it can penetrate (go into) the most stony heart, even as the magnetic force penetrates the glass.

Materials: Small, open cardboard box approximately 4" x 4" and a half inch deep, iron filings, and a piece of glass or plastic for the box lid. The purpose of a sealed box is to prevent the scattering and loss of the iron filings.

Procedure: Put filings in the box; then cover the box with the glass plate and tape securely. Place the magnet on the glass or beneath the box to observe the filings being attracted to it. Students should observe visually the movement of the filings towards the magnet and see how an invisible force can perform work at a distance from its visible source.

Notes: If your activity is done in an area where spilling iron filings is not a problem, you can simply sprinkle them on a piece of paper or into the lid of a stationery box, holding the magnet under the paper or lid.

You can buy iron filings from a school supply store or, if you don't mind them a little dirty, ask at a machine shop or an auto parts store that does some machine work.

Constellations with a slide projector

Objective: To develop skill in recognizing star constellations.

Spiritual lesson: As the stars gave direction for travelers in the past, the Bible is a safe guide for us.

Materials: Mounted slides from parents or a photographic dealer that are completely black, a sharp needle, and a book showing constellations.

Procedure: Make useful slides out of the film by punching holes in the pattern of the desired constellation.   Larger holes should be punched for brighter stars and holes for red stars may be covered with red cellophane tape.   As slides are projected on a screen or viewed on a light table, students will observe and identify the constellation or stars. Aluminum foil mounted on 2" x 2" cardboard frames may be similarly used.

Constellations in a box

Objective: To develop skill in recognizing star constellations.

Spiritual lesson: The more we study the stars, the easier it will be to identify them.   Just as more Bible study makes truth easier to identify.

Materials: Cardboard box, several dark pieces of paper or aluminum foil the size of the end of the box.

Procedure: Leave the cover on the box. Cut a window in one end and punch a peep hole in the other. Cover the window end with paper having holes punched to represent star patterns. Students view the star patterns by holding the window end to a light source and looking through the peep hole. Punched paper mounted in cardboard frames allows easy exchange for studying different constellation patterns.

How to slow down a frog

Objective: To observe a cold-blooded organism under normal conditions and to compare its behavior when its metabolic system has been slowed down.

Spiritual lesson: We are easily controlled if we are spiritually asleep.

Materials: Refrigerator or ice chest, and one, but preferably two, live frogs purchased from a pet store, bait shop, or biological supply house.

Procedure: Keep one frog in a cage or a box with high sides. Cool a second frog to between 40 and 50 degrees F by placing it in a glass jar and putting the jar in the refrigerator. This frog should be placed on top of wet paper towels in the jar, and the jar lid should have holes punched in it from the inside to prevent injury to the frog. A tray of water should be provided for the control frog (the one at room temperature). After one or two hours, remove the "cold" frog. Gently poke it with a broom straw or pencil just in front of the hind legs; move your hand rapidly toward it with a waving motion; and attempt to turn it upside down. Do the same to the control frog.

After the demonstration, return the cold frog to room temperature by placing it in water slightly warmer than room temperature.

Results: Students should observe that temperature affects a frog's behavior and reaction to stimuli. The cold frog will exhibit almost no response to stimulation, while the warm frog will be lively and attempt to escape. Students will observe that the refrigerated frog, when returned to room temperature, behaves "normally."

Note: Hands should be washed with soap after handling frogs or cleaning their cage.

A vibrating string

Objective: Students will observe how the sound made by a vibrating string changes when it is loosened or tightened.

Spiritual lesson: For our characters to vibrate with the true pitch of God's love, they must be "in tune" to His will.

Materials: A guitar or other stringed instrument.

Procedure: Have the students pluck a string as its peg is turned to tighten or loosen it.

Students will observe that tightening the string raises its pitch. The opposite effect is observed when the string is loosened.

You may explain frequency as the number of times the string swings one way, the other way and back each second. Of course it goes too fast to see. The A in the middle of the piano, for example, has a frequency of 440 vibrations per second. Pitch is what we hear. Frequency is what we could count if we could find a way to count that fast for a second.

Safety note: A string may break while being tightened. Children should wear eye protection and keep their faces at a distance from the strings. A string may be dangerous when it is tightened more than a little beyond its correct pitch.

For more experimentation: Note how the pitch will change when the length of the vibrating part of a string is changed. If you use an instrument, notice also how the weight (or thickness) of a string affects the pitch.

Make your own equipment: A rubber band around a book may not be very musical, but it's easy to "make" and use. Just stretch the rubber band around the book and put a pencil under it as shown in the illustration.

What you eat makes a difference

Objective: Students will observe how a natural wholesome diet is superior to one consisting of highly refined foods.

Spiritual lesson: One can only grow to be like Christ if what he receives into his body and mind are wholesome and Christlike.

Materials: Two very young laboratory rats, separate housing for each rat, other supplies for the keeping of laboratory animals, wood shavings, watering devices, refined foods (white bread, highly sugared dry cereal, candy, etc.) and wholesome foods (whole wheat bread, whole grain cereals, fruit, vegetables).

Method: (1) The rat cages must be thoroughly cleaned at least once a week, completely replacing the bedding. If needed, clean the cages more often. (2) Rats should have a good supply of fresh water at all times. (3) One rat should be given the "wholesome diet" and the other the "refined diet". Food discarded by the animals should be removed from the cages to prevent spoilage. (4) Keep a journal for each rat recording its condition each week. Items which especially should be observed are: weight, length, condition of fur, nose and eyes, and temperament.

Note: It is usually better to terminate this experiment before any conditions become serious. It might be mentioned that rat diets need not exactly parallel those for humans. For example, rotting meat is ideal for a vulture but not for humans.

Feeling for paper clips

Objective: To emphasize the sense of feeling in the fingers and to develop skills in observation.

Spiritual lesson: Jesus can take bad habits out of our lives if we ask Him to, and if we cooperate with Him. Another lesson: Consider the complexity of the God-given observation ability.

Materials: A bowl, two cups of oatmeal, 10 to 20 paper clips, and a blindfold.

Procedure: Mix the oatmeal and paper clips in the bowl. Blindfold a student. Place the bowl on his or her lap and measure the time it takes to find all the paper clips. Allow the student to do the experiment again to see if practice shortens the time needed.

Activities requiring greater observation skill are to separate three kinds of beans, or to find a certain coin in a mixture of other size coins.

Point to the sound

Objective: To show through observation that two ears are better than one in pointing out a source of sound.

Spiritual lesson: We need clear, open communication with the Lord to hear what He has to tell us.

Materials: A blindfold and two pencils.

Procedure: Blindfold a child without covering his or her ears. Then walk around the room and tap pencils together. The child sits in the center of the room and points in the direction from which he hears the sound. Repeat the process, but have the child put a finger in one ear.

Results: In the first situation the child should be able to correctly point in the direction of the sound. When one ear is plugged, his directions will be mixed up, and he will feel unsure of his responses.

Note of interest: A clock may be ticking on the wall, a kettle may be humming on the stove and someone may knock on the door. We are able to hear them all at once. We may also select the sound we want to listen to and concentrate on, in effect blocking out the others.

Erosion

Objective: To have students observe and discuss erosion.

Spiritual lesson: If we continually subject ourselves to undesirable influences, our Christian characters can be eroded. If we cover ourselves with Christ's life we will be protected.

Materials: Disposable aluminum pie pan, small stones, bottle caps or similar objects, and a spray bottle.

Procedure: Fill the pie pan with moist, moderately packed soil. Place the small objects on the soil. Tilt the pie tin slightly to facilitate run-off. Use the spray bottle to simulate conditions of rain on the soil. The light spray on the tilted pie pan will cause the soil to erode (run off). However, where the surface is protected, it will stand higher than the surrounding area. If convenient, a larger outdoor area and a sprinkler may be used with clumps of grass or leaves to protect the soil.

Matches

Objective: To develop observation skills by having the students identify and name properties of a wooden match before and after burning.

Spiritual lesson: We need to develop skills of observation so we can better understand the Lord and His word.

Materials: Wooden matches.

Procedure: Have the students make a list of observations about the wooden match. Let them hold it and encourage them to use as many senses as they can except the sense of taste. Then ask them the following questions: (1) What color is it? (2) Does it have an odor? (3) What is its shape and size? (4) What is its texture?

Then burn the match and have them record their observations while the match is burning and after it has finished. Students should compare their lists. Usually they will discover that others observed things they did not. More is usually accomplished through cooperation than through competition.

Note: Students must be *closely* *supervised* and cautioned *not* to play with matches.

Kindling temperatures

Objective: To observe the effect increasing the temperature has on starting a flame.

Spiritual lesson: Your love can warm someone's heart but it may take a little time to get the fire burning.

Materials: A candle and matches. A watch may also be used.

Procedure: (1) Oxygen (from the air) is needed to make fire. But notice that, in the presence of plenty of air, the candle does not start burning. (See the activity, "What happens to a lighted candle when covered?") Discuss what it is about a lighted match that could cause the candle flame to start. (2) Slowly move a lighted match closer and closer to the wick to see how close it´ needs to be to start the flame. Then blow out the candle and let it cool. (3) Move a lighted match directly up to the wick, but keep it there for only a short time, removing it before the flame starts. Then repeat for increasingly longer periods of time until the candle lights. You may also want to measure the time it actually takes to raise the temperature of the wax in the wick to make it vaporize and catch fire (ignite).

Observing / 28

Note: If a lighted match is placed in the smoke stream of an extinguished candle flame, the fire can "jump" an inch or so to reignite the candle.

Definition: The kindling temperature of a substance is the temperature at which it will ignite.

Practical lesson: The most common method of stopping a fire is to put water on it. This cools the material to below the kindling temperature and the burning stops. You may also note that a match laid on a piece of aluminum foil (which conducts away the heat) goes out.

Adopt a tree

Objective: The students will observe characteristics, growth patterns and seasonal changes of a tree.

Spiritual lesson: We should desire to become better acquainted with people in the same way we did the tree. We should see them as individuals. Usually the more we can observe and understand about a person, the more easily we can understand and love him or her.

Materials: Record book and a tree.

Procedure: Find a tree close by and have the children "adopt" it. Have them record everything they can about it. What kind is it? How tall is it? What is its circumference? Does it have buds? Do all branches grow the same length in one season? Is the number of leaves on a branch related to how much it grows? etc.

Periodically have the children visit the tree and record new observations.

The tree's height may be determined by comparing it to nearby buildings or the use of simple proportions. If the shadows of the tree and of a meter stick are measured, then the height of the tree is found by dividing the length of the meter stick by the length of its shadow and multiplying this result by the length of the tree's shadow.

Seed grower

Objective: The student will develop skills in observation by watching a seed in the process of germination.

Spiritual lesson: God gives life to the seed just as He gives physical and spiritual life to people.

Materials: Clear drinking glass, sheets of absorbent paper such as paper toweling or blotting paper, seeds, and water.

Procedure: Wet the paper and roll it into a cylinder, placing it inside the glass. Then place the seeds between the glass and the blotter, about a half inch from the bottom. Fill the glass to the level of the seeds but do not cover them. Add water occasionally to prevent their drying. Change the water every day. Have the students record their observations. The interior of the cylinder may be filled with tissue paper or wadded newsprint to hold the seeds firmly against the glass.

Seed embryos

Objective: To observe the living part of seeds.

Spiritual lesson: All life is a gift from the Creator. He has placed life in the seed.

Materials: Several large seeds such as peanuts, lima beans and peas; and a sharp knife.

Procedure: Split the seeds open to find the little plants inside.   Describe them.   For young children or if supervision is inadequate, try splitting the seeds without the knife or split them ahead of time for the students.   Also, a cutting board would be a good idea to protect tables or desks.   Soak the seeds overnight to make them easier to handle.

Pulse detector

Objective: To observe an effect of the heart-beat.

Spiritual lesson: Sin is like our pulse; it is sometimes so subtle that it is hard to detect.   But through the study of God's word we will have the equipment to detect it.

Materials: Wooden kitchen matches, and thumb tacks.

Procedure: Poke a thumb tack into the match and place the head of the tack on the thumb side of the upturned wrist as shown in the photograph.   The

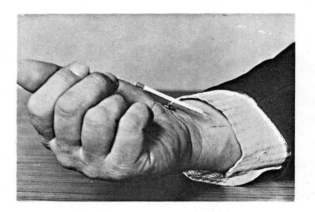

match will go up and down with the heart beat. You can count the heart beats per minute.

Why the blood moves the match: To see how the sudden bursts of pressure from the heart cause the movement of the blood vessels, hook up a garden hose and watch it while turning the water on and off quickly.

See also: The activity entitled, "Measuring pulse rate."

Measuring

Emulsified vegetable oil

Objective: The students will develop skills in measuring and, where possible, recognize that we measure so we can repeat our successes.

Spiritual lesson: Like droplets of oil in an emulsion, the message of God's love is to go to every nook and cranny in all the world.

Ingredients: One egg, three cups of vegetable or cooking oil, two teaspoons of lemon juice, salt.

Procedure: At medium speed, beat the egg until sticky. Then add the oil, a few drops to begin with, stirring constantly and increasing the oil gradually. Add two teaspoons of lemon juice after a cup or two of oil has been used, then more oil until all of the oil is used. The emulsion should be smooth and quite thick. Salt to taste and use as margarine. If too much oil is used, use the mixture as a creamy salad dressing. The idea is to spread tiny droplets of oil evenly through the egg yolks. The mixture should be refrigerated.

Question the students about whether the egg or the oil is the emulsifying agent. Having the students make smaller quantities and experiment with different amounts of ingredients helps them see the importance of measuring. If they did discover a better proportion, they would want or need to reproduce it. This emphasizes the need for careful lab notes.

Note: Raw eggs often carry salmonella and other disease germs. Lethicin is the substance in eggs which makes emulsion possible. You may wish to use it instead of eggs. It would be available from a health food store or a drug store.

Measurement of area

Objective: To give students the idea that units of measure are determined by convenience and tradition.

Spiritual lesson: We should not judge others. God has only one standard, the righteousness of Christ.

Materials: A small square of cardboard, a larger square that will allow the smaller one to fit into it nine times so that its area is 9 square units.

Procedure: Give the students each the small cardboard square and then the larger. Tell them that the smaller square is their measuring unit. Ask them to find the area of the larger one by finding out how many times the smaller one can be fitted into it. Have them mark off the smaller on the larger square with pencil lines. Then make other shapes and have them measure the area.

Example: Give your students two cardboard rectangles, one 6 x 4, and the other 8 x 3, and ask them if they are the same size. They will usually say no. Then have them measure carefully with their small measuring squares. Advanced students should be encouraged to measure triangles and irregular shapes. Suggest that they make up their own rules of measuring, such as, "When measuring odd shapes, if the little measuring square covers less than half of the space to be covered near the edge, then do not count it. If it is greater than half, count it."

Hidden space

Objective: To help children develop a sense of when to measure by volume and when to measure by weight.

Spiritual lesson: We have just so much time in our lives. We need to make the best use of it, and fill it with only good things.

Materials: A large beaker or glass, large marbles or marble-size stones, sand or BBs, and water.

Procedure: Place the marbles in the clear container and ask the students if it is full. They will likely say yes. Then add the sand while shaking and ask again if it is full. This time they may be more careful, but likely they again will say that it is full. Now pour in the water until the level reaches the top of the container and ask again.

Discussion: By volume, did the measure change when sand and water were added? By weight, did the measure change? This could be an appropriate point to explain: that all matter is mostly empty space, why metals expand, or the gas laws.

Measuring pulse rate

Objective: To show the effect of exercise on pulse rate. Students will be involved in measuring time.

Spiritual lesson: Just as the heart is able to supply the body with extra oxygen when needed, as long as we have been exercising regularly, so God is able to supply us with extra spiritual strength when it is needed and when we have kept close to Him.

Materials: A watch.

Method for finding the pulse: Find the bump on the palm side of the wrist, and feel the pulse with your fingers. The blood vessel you are looking for runs down the "valley" on the side of the bump toward the center of the wrist. (See the illustration.) Don't squeeze too hard or you will stop the blood and won't be able to feel it. The activity, "Pulse detector," shows an interesting, although not too practical, way of observing the pulse.

Bump on bone
Blood vessel

Procedure: Ask the students to measure their pulse rates while seated in the classroom. Students may first measure the number of beats in 15 or 30 seconds. Later measure the time required for a specific number of beats. This may be done several times. Of course the numbers would be different using the two methods, but students are usually surprised to learn that the rates are about the same.

Next have the students run up a flight of stairs and then figure their heart rate. Have them calculate the increase as they exercise more strenuously. Attempting to determine the time required for their heart to return to its normal rate will provide additional experience. Students will face interesting situations when asked to measure the heart rates of older people and pets.

After data have been gathered, they may be compared with weights, sizes, etc. Students will probably come to the generalization that the hearts of smaller animals beat faster.

Further investigation: Accuracy depends on how the pulse is measured. To learn more: (1) Count the pulse for a full minute and record the rate. (2) Count for half a minute and double the result to get the per-minute rate. (3) Check for a quarter of a minute and multiply by four. (4) Check the six- or fifteen-second rate several times. Heart rate varies, but this is not the only reason for differences. You may check for a full minute rate again. What did you learn about measuring? (Six and fifteen seconds are chosen because multiplication by ten and four are simple.)

Does soil quality matter?

Objective: Students will develop skills in measuring by demonstrating the progress of seeds in various types of soil.

Spiritual lesson: Our hearts are the soil for God's seeds of truth. If we listen to Him and obey Him, His seeds of truth will find good soil and will produce a healthy character.

Materials: Three containers for planting, some bean seeds and soil.

Procedure: Fill one container with rocky soil and one with potting soil. In a third, transplant some weeds in their own soil. Plant two bean seeds in each container. Keep them moist but be careful not to overwater. Have the students measure the growth rate and record related observations.

Is feeling a good measure?

Objective: To help students learn that feeling may not be accurate. (The method described as "simpler activity" may be better for younger children.)

Spiritual lesson: It is unsafe to trust feelings about spiritual things. We must study God's Word and listen to counsel of Christian friends.

Materials: A thermometer, four mixing bowels or styrofoam cups, sources of hot and cold water, and ice.

Procedure: (1) Ask students to mix water to make its temperature feel hot without burning. Fill one container about 2/3 full of this water. (2) Then using ice, put very cold water in a second container. (3) The instructor would mix water for the third container at an intermediate temperature and measure its temperature without telling the students. (4) Students may measure the temperatures of the hot and cold water. (5) Then they are asked to tell whether the water in the third container is hot or cold. They may also be asked to guess its temperature. They do this by putting one hand (or several fingers) into either the hot or cold water for maybe half a minute. One student feels the hot water and one the cold. Then they feel the "unknown" water.

Temperatures can be checked during or at the end of the experiment and reasons for changes explained.

Results: The intermediate water will feel hot to the cold-water student and cold to the hot-water student.

With only one student: (1) You may have the child measure and feel first the hot water and compare to the intermediate water. (2) Then the cold water could be felt and compared. (3) Finally, one hand is placed in the hot and the other in the cold, then both hands can be placed in the intermediate water.

Simpler activity: A student may try only the third step above and explain.

Change of state

Objective: To develop the concept that heat may do more than change temperature. It can also change a solid to a liquid.

Spiritual lesson: Ice, water and steam are different yet the same. How are the Father, Son and Holy Spirit alike while being different individuals?

Materials: A cooking utensil or large beaker, ice cubes, a heat source, a thermometer.

Procedure: (1) Put ice and the thermometer in the pan or beaker. Add enough cold water to cover the bulb of the thermometer. (2) Place your container on the heat source. Check the temperature every minute and record it in a table. Don't add heat too fast. (3) If you are using a weather thermometer, be careful to remove it before the fluid inside gets to the top. (4) Transfer your data (measurement information) to a graph as shown on the next page. You may need to extend the time axis if you have a large quantity of ice or a low heat source.

Time (Min.)	Temperature	Time (Min.)	Temperature
_____	_____	_____	_____
_____	_____	_____	_____
_____	_____	_____	_____
_____	_____	_____	_____
_____	_____	_____	_____

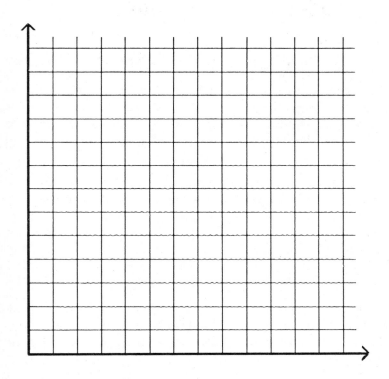

Time in minutes

Discussion: What do you see interesting about the graph? What did the heat do during the first part? During the second part? Heat is not the same as temperature. Heat is energy. We usually think of heat as causing the temperature of an object to increase. It also had another effect in this experiment.

Measuring up

Objective: To develop skill in measuring lengths.

Spiritual lesson: In this experiment, no card is right or wrong because it has longer or shorter lines than the others. In the same way, we should not judge people because they are different from us.

Materials: A set of cards with lines of varying length. Mark the cards individually with numbers for easy identification. Also have prepared sheets listing these numbers for recording results in a tabular form.

Procedure: Have the children measure the lines on the cards and record their lengths in inches, centimeters and millimeters as accurately as possible.

Note: Children do not automatically know how to measure with a ruler. Spend time discussing: (1) How to look squarely above the ruler so the object to be measured will correctly line up with the appropriate marks. (2) How to know the value of the smaller marks on the ruler since they don't have numbers by them. This will be particularly important when measuring in inches. (3) What to do when the end of the object falls between the marks. And so on.

Heat absorption

Objective: To observe how heat energy is absorbed.

Spiritual lesson: Those who choose the warmth of God's love receive the power to do right. See Malachi 4:2.

Materials: Very dry soil (use an oven if necessary), thermometers, two shallow cardboard boxes.

Procedure: Place in each box two inches of dry loose soil. Put one box in direct sunlight and the other in a shaded area. After an hour or more, have the children feel the soil in the lighted box with one hand and in the shaded box with the other. Using two thermometers (identical if possible) ask the students to measure and compare the temperatures. Place the bulbs of the thermometers at approximately the same depth in the soil.

A greater increase in temperature shows that more heat is absorbed as long as the two samples were of the same material and in the same quantity. Heat is a form of energy. Heavier materials tend to require more heat to raise their temperature a certain amount.

Mad measures

Objective: To introduce students to the concept of developing standards and measures.

Spiritual lesson: If our prayers and devotional routine sometimes seem boring, maybe it's because we aren't thinking of what we are saying. New ways and different words may help us mean what we say and say what we mean.

Materials: Objects such as crayons, pencils, a chalkboard, a desk, a window and a room.

Procedure: Ask your students to do the following: (1) measure the length of the classroom with their feet, (2) measure the rail of the chalkboard with their hands, (3) measure width of the desk top with a crayon, (4) measure the width of the window with a pencil. Have them record their results.

Then ask them questions such as the following: <1> If there are two-and-one-half crayons to a foot, how many feet wide is the desk-top? <2> If your pencil is twice as long as your hand, how many hands wide is the window? <3> If your foot equals ten inches, how many inches long would the room be? <4> If your hand equals a crayon, how many crayons long is the chalk tray?

Conclude by asking if they can see any advantage to a standard unit of measure (using feet and inches). Let them compare their results with one another to note differences. You may direct the discussion toward the metric system to discover in what ways it might be a better system for measurement.

For extra interest: (1) Read about the history of measurement in an encyclopedia. (2) Note how measurement is used for communication. A pencil plus a number, for example, can carry information about the length of a table top to another place. If pencils were a standard size and your friend in a distant city also had one, only the number and the word "pencil" would be needed to tell how long the table top is. How would this be like the way we use standard units of measure?
If you don't have access to an encyclopedia, look under "measurement" in a good dictionary.

Air currents

Objective: To have the students make an air current tester that shows how air moves. Measurement usually means placing a number value on some kind of quantity. In this case we are *detecting* air movement rather than *measuring* it.

Spiritual lesson: Air, like faith, is not always visible in its movement.

Materials: A drinking straw, a piece of paper about 3" x 4", a paper clip, a pencil, a pin, and tape.

Procedure: Flatten one inch at the end of the straw. Tape the paper to it. Push the pin through the middle of the straw and into the eraser of the pencil. Wiggle the straw a little so that it can turn easily around the pin. Flatten the other end of the straw. Slide the paper clip on the end. Pick up the pencil and see if the straw hangs level. If not, slide the paper clip back or forth until it is level.

Test the air currents in your room. Hold the tester over a warm place such as a lighted bulb or a sunny window sill. What happens to the paper? What made it move? Which way did it move? Hold the tester below the bottom of a refrigerator door or over some ice cubes. Which way does the cold air current move? Take the temperature readings in several places in the room. Record the results. Try your air current tester in those places. Compare the results with temperature readings.

A candle flame, balloons or feathers may also be used to detect air currents.

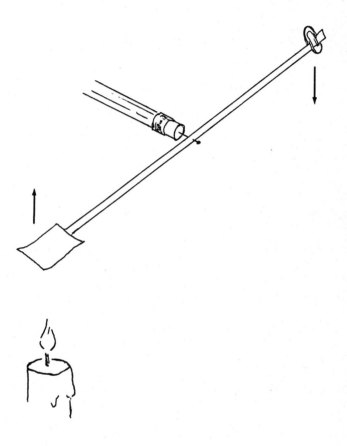

Air current detector

Fun with pumpkins

Objective: To examine a source of food and make scientific measurements.

Spiritual lesson: The pumpkin is one example of the bounty of good food provided for us by God.

Materials: A pumpkin for each student or group of students, kitchen knives, a scale calibrated in fractions of a pound or kilogram, baking utensils.

Procedure: Have the students weigh their pumpkins, measure the circumferences, then open them and count the seeds. Weigh the seeds and prepare the pumpkin for baking. The students will have fun measuring the pumpkins and comparing them, measuring the ingredients for the pie, and eating the results.

Pumpkin carving should be attempted only by older students under supervision. One pumpkin may make several pies.

Milk to cheese

Objective: To have the students develop skills in measuring by making cottage cheese.

Spiritual lesson: The Lord mixes His love into our lives to makes something useful out of us.

Materials: Two quart jars, a bowl, a small glass, a funnel, a square of cheesecloth, a teaspoon, one pint of skim (or other) milk, one rennet tablet (available at food stores).

Procedure: Pour the milk into the jar and place the jar in the bowl full of warm water. Dissolve the rennet tablet with a teaspoon of warm water. Stir the mixture into the jar of warm milk. Let the milk stand for about fifteen minutes until it looks like the white of a soft-boiled egg. When you stir it with a spoon, there will be bits of white in a greenish liquid. Wait until the white bits are firm, and then put the cheesecloth over the top of the funnel and pour the curdled milk through cheesecloth and funnel into the other jar. The white part will stay in the cheesecloth and the greenish liquid or "whey" will go into the empty jar. Salt and eat the white curds. Dispose of the whey.

Method options: (1) Also, cottage cheese may be formed by pouring boiling water into clabbered milk until whey forms. Let it stand for fifteen minutes and drain as above. (2) Buttermilk may be used as a culture instead of rennet. The mixture should set at about 70 °F for 10 to 12 hours. A comprehensive cookbook will give details on other methods.

Classifying

Kin count

Objective: To develop skills in classification by listing family members by relationship.

Spiritual lesson: No matter what we do or who we are, we will be classified by people.   We would want them to consider us reliable.

Materials: Lists of all relatives students know or can find out about.

Procedure: Have the students organize their lists by type—that is, cousins, uncles, aunts, etc.   When they have done this, write the total number of cousins, uncles, etc.   Write all the names and list them in order of frequency.

Tree identification

Objective: To classify pictures of fruit trees by the fruit they bear.

Spiritual lesson: People are known by the results of what they do, just as trees can be identified by the fruit they produce (Matt. 7: 15-20 and Prov. 20:11).

Materials: Fruit tree pictures cut from nursery catalogs.   If convenient, actual fruit may also be used.

Procedure: Have the child sort the pictures by identifying the fruit.   Pictures of orange trees, for example, would be placed by the orange.

An older child may enjoy preparing the exercise for a younger one.

An alternative exercise would be to sort pictures of trees with fruit and ones without (Luke 13:6-10).

Hierarchical classification

Objective: The students will learn skills in the process of ordering and differentiating between classes.

Spiritual lesson: Though people have different characteristics, they are still a part of the family of the Creator, just as the different varieties of roses are still members of the rose family.

Materials: A set of twelve pictures of flowers as follows: four pictures of yellow roses, four pictures of roses by all different colors (red, orange, pink, white), and four pictures of flowers other than roses.

Procedure: Spread the pictures on a table and instruct the children to put them together so that they are alike. General questions as to color or type of object may be helpful in guiding their thinking. Ask them the following questions: (1) If you make a bouquet putting all the flowers you have in it, would you use the yellow roses? (2) Would a bunch made of all the yellow roses be larger or smaller than a bunch made of all roses? (3) Are there more roses or more flowers? Why? (4) If you take all of the roses, will there be any flowers left? Why?

The singular class in class inclusion

Objective: The student will develop skills in classification by investigating problems that arise from the notion of a singular class.

Spiritual lesson: The Lord tells us the difference between right and wrong, but he allows us to choose for ourselves.

Materials: Pictures in sets of three—For example, three birds, three reptiles, three fish, etc. Two in each set need to be very similar and the third obviously dissimilar. For example, two may be of the same species but from a different view. The third may be of a larger or different species. Make up the sets by mounting the pictures on cards. For each set mark an X on the back side of the one that is "different."

Procedure: Tell the students to figure out which picture in each set has an X marked on the back. Don't refer to one picture being different. Just ask them to guess and check their ideas. When they find the marked one, place another set of pictures before them. Ask them to explain the reasoning behind their choice on successive sets and encourage them to construct a puzzle or a game using your material.

Multiple classification

Objective: The students will develop skills in classification by doing an activity involving multiple classification.

Spiritual lesson: All are created equal in value but different in talents. Each has been given a special talent to use for the Lord's work.

Information needed: Find out facts about the children such as: birth date, existence of siblings, favorite foods, hobbies, and clothing color.

Procedure: Students may be arranged in rows and columns in a double classification. If you gather your information with a questionnaire, the children can figure out more easily which characteristics you have used for classification. Explain to the students that in multiple classification each student may belong to two or more classes. An example would be an arrangement where the girls are seated on the left side of the room and boys on the right to form two classes of children. If those with birthdays in the spring and summer are in the front and those with birthdays in the fall and winter are towards the back, students can readily see they are classified as to both sex and season of birth.

For one student: Children working by themselves could arrange buttons according to size as the first level of classification and then according to the number of holes.

Seeds

Objective: The students will develop skills in classifying by being able to name and identify several wild plants by their seeds.

Spiritual lesson: Our habits are like seeds. We can choose which ones we wish to develop and those we wish to eliminate.

Materials: An area containing mature plants and two small boxes of soil (milk cartons cut in half lengthwise may be used.)

Procedure: Take the students for a walk through an area to collect seeds and note from what plants they come. Seeds and identifying labels may be kept together in small paper cups or zip-lock sandwich bags. Discuss why the plants might be useful or useless.
Plant one box with only "useful" seeds and in another mix both "useful" and "useless" seeds. Water the seeds and set in a place enhancing plant growth. Observe and note the difference between the two boxes. Have the students remove the weeds from the mixed box. A couple of handfuls of moist potting soil placed in the bottom of zip-lock bags make excellent growth chambers. Do not place sealed bags in direct sunlight as they may overheat.

Note: Wild seeds may be mixed with seeds from mature fruits and vegetables from the garden. Students may discover the arbitrary nature of different classifications.

Investigating ways to extinguish fire

Objective: The student will develop skills in classification by defining ways to put out fires.

Spiritual lesson: We need to read our Bibles and pray so we can stay close to God and so that Satan cannot put out our fire of love for God.

Materials: One large candle, matches, one small test tube or jar, and an eye dropper.

Procedure: Have the students light the candle and describe what they see. Then have them invert the test tube over the candle and record the results. Then re-light the candle and blow on it and record the results. Relight the candle again but this time put a drop of water on the flame. They may try several other ways of extinguishing a candle. Ask them what made the candle go out. Have them note common elements, then create a classification by categorizing the different methods.

You may also wish to extinguish the candle flame in other ways such as pinching the wick, cutting the wick off with a pair of scissors, surrounding the flame with a spiral of copper wire, pouring carbon-dioxide on the flame, or using salt, baking powder, or a fire extinguisher.

Carbon dioxide may be obtained by adding two teaspoons of baking soda to one-half cup of vinegar in the bottom of a large soft-drink bottle. The gas formed is carbon dioxide and may be poured from the bottle.

Note: Students should be cautioned NOT to play with fire or matches, and should be given basic safety instructions for using fire.

Food groups

Objective: The students will be able to identify foods of several groups according to a selected number of characteristics such as sour, sweet or salty. Identification differs from classification in that identification requires pre-established groups.

Spiritual lesson: Taste helps us enjoy food, but good taste does not mean the food is good for us. In the same way, we must do things because they are right not just because they are fun (Prov. 14:12).

Materials: Cheese, banana, apple, olive, lemon, onion, carrot and other foods cut into small pieces, tooth picks, paper plates, and a blindfold.

Procedure: Select one child to be blindfolded. Have him hold his nose as he holds out his tongue to have some food placed on it. Ask him how it tastes and then which food he thought it was. Without holding his nose repeat the process. Continue with the same food or something different, asking him the same questions. Continue using different students until the food supply is exhausted. In each case use the classes the students use such as sour, salty, sweet, bitter, etc. Children will realize that smelling and taste are related as well as learning the differences between classification and identification. Colored toothpicks may help students viewing from a distance.

Caution: Students should be told NOT to use laboratory equipment for food or drink.

Notes: Experimenters should be aware that different zones on the tongue are differently sensitive to sweet, sour, bitter, etc. Avoid a common mistake of telling students what to expect. Blending could reduce the "texture" clue to place more emphasis on taste. Many textbooks overstate the smelling factor saying that a person cannot differentiate between foods such as apples, potatoes, and onions when blind folded and with nose plugged.

Skin inside the nose (called the olfactory mucous membrane) is active in smelling and tasting. Smoking damages this area, blocking most of the delicate flavors and odors. Sweet and salty tastes detected by the tongue are still active and tend to be overused by smokers tired of "tasteless" food.

States of matter

Objective: The students will review properties of solids, liquids, and gases, and they will identify substances accordingly.

Spiritual lesson: Just as we may not realize that Silly Putty® acts like a liquid as well as a solid, so we often misunderstand people. We should not judge.

Materials: A package of Silly Putty.

Procedure: First review the properties of a solid, a liquid, and a gas. Have students record their observations as they play with Silly Putty. Place the words "solid" and "liquid" on the board and ask the class to tell you the properties of each and write them under the words. Then ask them to describe the properties of Silly Putty. Categorize all properties discovered by the students. Conclude by calling attention to the fact that the Silly Putty has certain properties of both states of matter.

The classification game

Objective: To use all five senses in classifying.

Spiritual lesson: If we study our Bibles enough we will be able to distinguish between right and wrong just like we can distinguish between solids and liquids.

Materials: A rock, a marble, a pencil, three beans, three pieces of rock candy, one ruler, one small bottle of syrup, one small bottle of milk, one small bottle of soda water, one small bottle of vegetable oil, and/or other objects to be classified; and three boxes marked A, B, and C for sorting. Begin your demonstration with all the objects except the three labeled boxes in a larger carton.

Procedure: Remove the rock, feel it, press it, and put it into the box labeled A. Remove the bottle of vegetable oil and move it around so that the children see the oil move. Then place it in box B. Avoid stating "rules" to the game or in any way indicating "right" or "wrong" responses. Box C will be used only if students see a different way of classification. Repeat the process with the marble and the bottle of milk. Next, take out the pencil and press it and hit it against the table. Ask the students which box they think it should belong in. Ask them to play the classification game with you.

Discussion: After the solids have been placed into box A and the liquids into box B, ask the children to tell you why they were put into the different boxes and have them describe what characteristics the objects have in common. Also ask what kinds of things might belong in box C.

Sun, moon, and planets

Objective: While studying the solar system, to describe planets and order them according to size or with respect to their distance from the sun.

Spiritual lesson: Just as the sun is the light and center of our solar system, so Christ should be the light and center of our lives.

Materials: Several spherical balloons (colored).

Procedure: Prepare a balloon for each planet and for the sun and moon. Make the balloons correspond in size from small to large in the order of the sizes of the celestial bodies they represent. Then place them in order according to the distance from the sun. You may also have the students show how the moon orbits the revolving earth and how the earth and other planets rotate around the sun. Ask your students to hold the balloons and go through the appropriate movements around the "sun." The "moon" should remember that it always faces the earth, while the earth travels around the sun.

Older students may wish to consider the factor of time and allow the distance taken for one step every five seconds to indicate distances traveled during the passing of one earth day or week.

All sorts

Objective: To develop skills in classification by having student identify and discriminate among buttons.

Spiritual lesson: Although humans, like buttons, may be classified into various groups, all are valuable.

Materials: Have children bring as many old buttons as they can. Buttons may be purchased inexpensively from service organizations.

Procedure: Allow the student to sort the buttons by shape, size, color, texture, and number of holes. As they are sorted into groups, many will be found to belong to more than one group, indicating the need for a more complex classification system.

Getting hooked up right

Objective: To teach skills related to classification by having the student identify bones.

Spiritual lesson: Our bones cannot be seen from our outward appearance, but they provide the firm structure and support for our bodies. Without them we would be worthless. In a similar way our Bible is our spiritual foundation, our support for all of life.

Materials: Wire, hooks or other fasteners, a Halloween skeleton, paper, and scissors.

Procedure: Make a "spooky" biology chart by getting a Halloween skeleton and making attachable identifications (for the different bones.) Wire, hooks or other fasteners could be used to attach labels and facilitate relabeling by different students.
Alternatively students may wish to make a paper skeleton and identify the major bones. Poster board could be used.

The null class

Objective: To emphasize the nature of the null class.

Spiritual lesson: Someone who enjoys a certain thing like hiking finds it easy to be friends with other people who like the same things. Those who become friends with Jesus begin to agree with what He says is important.

Materials: Science picture cards of several classes of objects such as plants, minerals, or animals.

Procedure: (1) Place the cards in front of the student and tell him to put them into groups or classify them the way he chooses. (2) Then ask him to make another classification using only two groups. Ask for the reasoning behind these choices. (3) Finally, ask your students to think of a class that none of the pictures could be put into. This is called a null class.

Communicating

Blind walk

Objective: For two people to communicate by words and touch while one of them is unable to see. Also to better appreciate the value of sight.

Spiritual Lesson: We can be thankful for our Bibles and the Holy Spirit which are given to guide us safely on the heavenward path.

Materials: Blindfolds.

Procedure: Children can test the statement, "Senses give us information," by going on blind walks. To do this, one child is blindfolded while another takes him or her on a walk, either indoors or outdoors. The leader must tell the walker when to step down or up, when to listen, when to touch the bark of a tree or bend down to touch grass and the like. The leader must be particularly attentive, careful and communicative in order to avoid accidents. After a while, partners reverse roles.

Ask (1) what information can be received without the sense of sight, and (2) in the experiment, how other senses helped.

Note: It may be well to point out that only a small part of the sensory information a person receives is through communication.

Caution: Blindfolds may spread diseases such as pinkeye.

Discussion: God, too, speaks to us through our senses.

Find your rock

Objective: To develop skills in observing by becoming aware of the different characteristics of rocks. Then to communicate the observation clearly.

Spiritual Lesson: We are all unique individuals with characteristics special to God.

Materials: A collection of rocks each marked with a number.

Procedure: Place a collection of rocks in the center of a circle of students. Each selects a rock and is given a few minutes for observation and for recording the number on the rock. The rocks are passed around the circle and are then placed out of sight.

The activity may be continued as a game. A student is chosen and asked to describe his or her unseen rock. Then if the rock you bring out of hiding according to the description turns out to be the correct one, this student becomes the new leader. Otherwise the real owner becomes the leader.

Another way to continue would be to bring the rocks back into sight placing them number-side down in the circle of students. Then the owner of each rock could describe it without pointing. You would choose a rock fitting the description. The identity could then be verified, and the process continued with the other students.

Colorful leaf collections

Objective: To make leaf silhouettes on paper and explore the artistic mode of communication.

Spiritual Lesson: Our lives can, with Christ's assistance, make a beautiful imprint on the life of another person.

Materials: Leaves, plain or colored sheets of paper, tempera paints, a tooth brush, newspaper, and straight pins.

Procedure: Cover with newspaper the area to be used, then carefully pin the leaf or leaves to the paper. Dip the toothbrush into the paint and gently shake off the excess. Then by moving the thumb (or another object such as a table knife blade) across the brush, splatter bits of paint over the area, especially around the edges of the leaf. Wait until the print has dried to remove the leaf.

Providing leaves of different species and requesting students to identify and label their prints can stress the importance of plant names in scientific communication. Print pictures make an attractive bulletin board.

Using a frame, covered with screen wire, would cause less mess from stray paint spatters. Make the frame as illustrated, from boards three or four inches high. Dip the toothbrush in paint and move it across the screen to spatter the paper below. The rectangular shape of the frame would also produce attractive, unspattered borders for the prints.

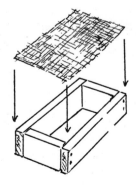

Germs don't like soap

Objective: To develop the children's communication skills through role play.

Spiritual Lesson: God sends the Holy Spirit to wash our hearts when we ask Him to cleanse us.

Materials: Assign the following names to students to act out certain characters: Sally Soap, Polly Person, Willie Water, and Jerry Germ.

Procedure: Have Polly Person stand in the middle of the room and have Jerry Germ sneak up to her and hug or hold onto her. Then have Willie Water and Sally Soap come up holding hands, and wipe away the germ pushing him to a far corner of the room.

To develop communication skills allow the students to elaborate on the theme by providing a script to be read telling what is really going on when the soap and water are used for personal hygiene.

Note: Washing with soap usually "exiles" germs without killing them. The play could be expanded to include another scene where Sam Sunlight (student with flashlight) attacks germs producing their dramatic death.

String-and-can telephone

Objective: The student will better understand characteristics of sound conductive materials and may see that a communication system can lose its ability to carry a message.

Spiritual Lesson: For God to hear our prayers, we must maintain a tight connection. This means we must keep a close relationship with Him.

Materials: Two empty cans and twine or thin wire 10 to 20 feet long depending on the size of the room.

Procedure: Puncture the closed end of each can. Connect the cans by putting the ends of the string through the holes. Knot the string so it will not pull out of the cans. A child on each end of the "telephone" talks and listens through the cans and string.

Discussion: Ask the participants how well they were able to communicate when the string was loose and when it was tight. Ask why they think sound traveled through the tight string and what other factors might influence the effectiveness of the system.

If appropriate, talk about the nature of sound waves and how sound is transmitted though the air. The can-and-string system transmits sound in a similar way. The sound vibrations may be explained as a series of little pushes sent along the line. The pushes tighten and loosen the string, making the can on the other end vibrate and reproduce the sound.

Flip books

Objective: Children will learn communication skills by making a cartoon flip book presenting a scientific law in reverse.

Spiritual Lesson: As each picture in the flip book contributes to the overall idea, each thoughtful act and kindly deed performed builds character.

Materials: Paper, pencils, and/or crayons.

Procedure: Have each student pick an aspect of a natural law and make a flip book on "breaking" that law. For example, trees growing backwards or apples falling up. To make a flip book, take a small stack of blank paper or cards. Then draw a picture on the first page, keeping it simple without a background. Then on each successive page, trace the previous picture but make a slight variation. To use the book, flip the pages. To reverse the motion, flip from the other end of the stack. Each student will be eager to share his or her book with class members.

Discussion: Talking about time-lapse photography can help students realize that scientific communication may require more than written words. Through time-lapse photography the opening of a flower bud can be communicated more thoroughly and clearly than by any other means.

Motion pictures work like the flip books and are interesting to discuss. Video motion is a little more complex. A change is made at any point on the screen as the electron beam returns in its cycle of tracing the whole screen line by line.

Original story problems

Objective: To develop skills in communication by writing arithmetic word problems.

Spiritual Lesson: God can lead us to an answer for every problem of life.

Materials: Paper, pencil, and old magazines.

Procedure: Each child will write an original story problem to be illustrated with a picture from a magazine.   The picture is mounted and the problem is written on one side of a uniform size sheet.   The solution is written on the back.   After each child has made a contribution, fasten the sheets together to make a book.
You may want to ask your children to make problems about a specific topic such as why we have so much litter, or how we can conserve energy.
Students may enjoy solving each other's problems.

Making peanut butter sandwiches

Objective: To develop skills in communication by giving and following directions.

Spiritual Lesson: It is important that our lives accurately reflect Bible truths so that they direct others to the Saviour.

Materials: A loaf of bread, a jar of peanut butter, a jar of jam, and a knife.

Procedure: Ask the children to write out directions for making a peanut butter and jelly sandwich. Then collect the directions and proceed to make the sandwiches following them literally. For example, if the students make no mention of using a knife, use a finger to spread the peanut butter. If they were not explicit about covering only one side of the bread, then cover both sides and edges. You may decide to have the one who wrote the instructions eat the sandwich.

Finally have the class make a set of instructions that are concise, accurate and complete. While making sandwiches is not considered a scientific activity, it illustrates the need for writing clear, unambiguous directions in terms that others readily understand.

Discussion: In actual direction-giving situations, people don't need to explain absolutely everything because those following the instructions already understand part of what they need to do. Discuss how to know when enough has been said for clear directions, and when too much is better than not enough.

Using Numbers

Find the largest

Objective: To use numerical comparisons to find the largest tree, leaf or other natural object.

Spiritual lesson: The human mind is endowed with the power to discriminate between right and wrong. God planned that man should not make decisions from impulse, but from the evidence of comparing Scripture with Scripture.

Materials: List of objects in or around the school, such as pencils, books, trees, or pictures on the bulletin board which students can easily compare by measuring.

Procedure: Distribute lists to teams of two or three students and have them find the largest item in each given category. For older students, be more specific. For example, request that they find the tallest tree or that they find and measure the diameter breast high (DBH) of several specimens each, of different tree species.

Thinking fast

Objective: To use numbers for record keeping, and to test whether or not practice increases a person's speed in accomplishing certain tasks.

Spiritual lesson: Often students do not use their time well. Since life is made of time, the way we use it is very important to God. Even small amounts of time are valuable.

Help students realize that it may be necessary to slow down to do a good job. Being naturally slow is not sin! Frivolous talk, telling jokes and other ways of wasting time can be.

Materials: Sheets of paper with numbers written on them, some with the numbers in sequential order, and others with them randomly arranged; and a stop watch, or other instrument for measuring time in seconds.

Procedure: Students are given a paper with numbers and asked to touch the numbers in an ascending or descending order and to record the time required. Usually ten to twenty-five numbers per page is adequate. Older students may repeat the experiment several times and make a graph comparing the time required with the amount of practice.

A family tree

Objective: To use numbers and manipulatives to better understand the reproductive potential of plants and animals.

Spiritual lesson: If a single individual shares the message of God's love with two people and each of these shares with two others, and so on, then the great gospel commission: "Go ye into all the world" could be accomplished in a few weeks.

Materials: A large number of small identical objects to use as markers, cup, yeast, sugar and water.

Procedure: Give groups of students hypothetical problems such as: a bacterium divides in half to produce two "new" bacteria. One hour is needed for one generation. How many generations or hours would be needed to produce 64 individuals. Have the students simulate the process using the small objects. At the same time have them use a calculator to develop confidence in its use. Next, increase the target number and recalculate the number of generations. Eventually approach other types of reproduction where two individuals are needed as in human reproduction. Finally consider the case where one individual, such as a flowering plant, can produce thousands of offspring.

Add a small quantity of fresh yeast to a cup of warm sugar water and put it in a warm place where students can periodically observe the yeast's growth.

Something to think about: Each person living today has two parents, four grandparents, eight great grandparents, and so on. If a generation of humans is taken to be 30 years, then 600 years ago (20 generations back) each of us had 1,040,400 ancestors! That would mean that 600 years ago there were more than a million times as many people as there are today. Obviously there is an error in reasoning. Can you find it?

How big is big?

Objective: To use large numbers intelligently and to better understand the magnitude of large numbers encountered in measurements of time and distance.

Spiritual lesson: God's ideal for us is greater than we can imagine (Isa. 55:8, 9).

Materials: Typewriter and paper.

Procedure: Have the students type characters to fill most of a sheet of paper. Conveniently 50 rows of 80 characters each will give 4000 characters per page. Have the students use ditto or other means of rapid duplication to produce 250 identical pages. (Or simply take 250 sheets of blank paper imagining each of them to have 4000 characters). This will give a collection of one million characters. Students are then encouraged to find scientific facts involving large numbers and to translate the numbers found in terms of the collection of characters they have made.

As an alternative, you might ask students to count the words on a normal page from a book. They may multiply by five for the average word length to get the number of letters. Then have them see how many pages have words. Multiplying by that number gives them the number of letters in the entire book.

Large number comprehension

Objective: The students will gain skills in using numbers by learning to differentiate between large numbers.

Spiritual lesson: The fact that God has numbered the hairs on our heads shows us that He cares for us.

Materials: Sufficient square samples of grass.

Numbers / 80

Procedure: Have the children count the number of blades of grass in each square inch and take an average. Have them then multiply that average by 144 to find out the number of blades for a square foot. Then find out how much space is needed for a million blades of grass. To do this have them divide one million by the average in a square foot. For a billion blades of grass have them divide one billion by the same number.

In a similar activity, students could "count" the number of hairs on someone's head. They could count for one square centimeter and multiply by the estimated square centimeters of hair surface. Encourage them to devise a plan to make their work as easy as possible while keeping a degree of accuracy.

Notes: Either of these activities could require a considerable length of time. You may wish to simplify the first step of the grass density problem by counting for a typical square inch instead of finding an average. If students can figure out on their own what to do to find the area needed for a million blades, the mathematical process will make more sense for them.

Surface tension

Objective: To use numbers to facilitate record keeping and improve accuracy in predicting.

Spiritual lesson: For a time, we may be able to hide our wrongdoing from friends. However, if we continue in sin, even they will see wrong spilling over.

Materials: A small cup or glass, water, straight pins or paper clips, coins and a medicine dropper.

Procedure: Water's ability to stand above the top of a container is an example of surface tension. Have the students fill a small container with water. Then count the number of small objects as they are dropped into the container. To give practice in predicting, have the students estimate the number of objects required to break the surface tension and cause the water to overflow. Wild guessing is of little scientific value although it encourages student involvement. Students should be directed to predict as accurately as possible. For example, to say that more pins than paper clips would be required is a better statement before more adequate data are available than predicting that 100 pins will be required to make the water overflow.

Drops of water from a medicine dropper dropped on a coin can similarly be used. Ask what will happen when water is gently dropped on a coin, or to predict whether or not the number of drops needed to cause overflow will increase or decrease if coins of different size are used, or what happens if the coins are coated with wax, grease or oil.

Note: Salt or detergent may be added to the water to change the surface tension.

How the Egyptians built the pyramids

Objective: To measure and use numbers to arrive at an answer. In this exercise, most students will get an incorrect answer because they fail to consider all of the facts.

Spiritual lesson: We don't try to find answers to some problems because we think they are too difficult. God will help us do as much as we are really able if we ask.

Materials: Three or four rollers about three inches long and approximately an inch in diameter (dowel rod or sections cut from a broom handle), and a piece of wood three inches wide and six to eight inches long to represent the slabs used in building the pyramids of Egypt. (Thickness of the wood is unimportant.)

Procedure: Direct students to measure the circumference of the rollers (3" shown in the picture) and ask them, "How far will the slab move forward when the rollers make one revolution"? After they have made a commitment, allow them to model the movement of slabs for a pyramid. Students will normally predict the distance moved to be equal to the circumference of the rollers. Actually the slab will move twice the circumference. Students fail in predicting the correct result since they fail to realize that the centers of the rollers also move forward.

Although most history books subscribe to the above theory that the Egyptians used rollers to move the huge stones from the quarry to the site where they were used, it seem more logical that the Egyptians quarried the stones cylindrically, rolled the stone cylinders to the location, and then carved them to fit.

How old am I?

Objective: To determine the age of trees or box turtles by counting rings or ridges.

Spiritual lesson: For everything there is a time or season.

Materials: Sanded and polished cross sections of tree trunks, box turtle shells, tree branches, or other natural objects for which age is easily determined.

Procedure: Have the students count the number of rings in the cross sections of trees, the number of ridges of the abdominal scute of box turtles and/or the bundle scars on young twigs or branches. Invite the students from other classrooms in your school to visit your room and have the children in your class guess how old they are. An age-guessing booth as part of a parents' night program will provide fun and practice. For turtles and other animals the relationship of size to known ages will generate ideas about interpolation and extrapolation. The activity can be extended to find out how scientists determine the ages of many things.

Numbers, numbers everywhere

Objective: To make children aware of the wide variety of ways numbers are used.

Spiritual lesson: In life we tend to find what we look for. If we seek God, we will find Him. He is involved in our everyday life just as numbers are.

Procedure: Separate newspapers into enough single sheets for each student to have one. Mark a big "X" on the side they are not to use. Fold the sheets and distribute them. Ask them to find and circle all the numbers. Then have them count (a) all the numbers written in words, (b) all written in digits, (c) all the numbers showing amounts of money, (d) all the numbers greater than 100, and (e) all the numbers showing fractions.

Students will realize now that we use numbers in everyday activities. You may ask them, also, to think of ways numbers are used in science. They can make lists or simply discuss the ways.

Note: Newsprint ink rubs off. It may be necessary to clean the desk tops after this activity.

Nature number walk

Objective: To make children aware of the variations, patterns and designs in nature.

Spiritual lesson: Pattern and regularity are important in God's great universe. As we choose to fit into His beautiful plan, He will help us be faithful.

Materials: Walking area (a neighborhood or nature trail), a paper numbered from 1 to 10 or 12 with several blank lines following each number.

Procedure: Take a nature walk and ask students to make lists of natural objects that come in groups of each of the numbers. Three- and four-leaf clovers could be listed. The numbers 1 to 6 are the easiest to find. For example, the number of large veins in a leaf or the petals on a flower. Larger numbers are frequently found as the number of leaves produced in a year's growth on a twig or the number of leaflets on compound leaves. Students should be encouraged to look for numbers that are rather consistent such as the three leaves of poison ivy.

Overcrowded living

Objective: To demonstrate some of the effects of overcrowding.

Spiritual lesson: God gives us all the same amount of time every day. Careful planning is best, not trying to do too many or too few things.

Materials: Space and materials for growing plants from seed. (Seed companies will often give seeds to teachers in the fall of the year.)

Procedure: In uniform sized containers, plant varying numbers of seeds. The largest number should be a situation where each seed is touching another. Provide uniform care for all containers. Students should keep records showing when the sprouts break ground, and they should periodically measure the plants' height. The plants' competition for light, water and nutrients will be seen.

Discuss: (1) The value of country living, (2) effects overcrowding might have on people, and (3) actions that might reduce the problems from situations we cannot change.

By two's

Objective: To develop skills in pattern recognition using patterns in numbers on a calendar.

Spiritual lesson: Why were the disciples sent out by two's? A possible suggestion is that they complimented each other, where one was weak the other may have been strong. Also, God used each as a channel of spiritual strength and courage for the other.

Materials: A monthly calendar.

Procedure: Have the students choose a 2x2 square of dates and ask them to find the sum along the two diagonals. They will be surprised to find them equal. Ask them to show that it is true for any 2x2 square selected. This activity teaches orderly investigation. Extend the activity to 3x3 and 4x4 squares of dates. Can a month have a 5x5 square? Which months and what years?

Ask the students to search for additional patterns or to verify the statement that the middle number of any three in a row horizontally, vertically, or diagonally is the average of the other two. The calendar is obviously an orderly sequence of numbers, but few students will have seen the obvious patterns. Sequences of four numbers are such that the sum of the first and last equals the sum of the middle two. When students have "caught onto the patterns", be certain to use them in making predictions.

Percentage germination

Objective: To use numbers to compare seed quality.

Spiritual lesson: Just as God knows how each seed will produce or fail, so He also knows which of us will produce or fail spiritually, but does not force us in either direction. Just as He nourishes each seed, which has no choice, even more so does He nurture and care for us who DO have the power of choice.

Materials: Seeds and paper towel or burlap squares 6 to 8 inches on a side.

Procedure: Count out between 25 and 100 seeds. Place them between moistened paper or burlap. If rolled and placed in sealed plastic bags, much less care is required. Have the students check on the seeds daily, counting the number of seeds that germinate. When no more seeds germinate for two or three days, the percentage germination is calculated by dividing the number that germinated by the original number counted for testing. Students may experiment with heat and light to determine their effect on germination rate and success. Certain lettuce seeds may be switched on and off by treatments of red and infrared lights.

Inferring

Growing seeds

Objective: To infer that some green plants need light energy to grow.

Spiritual lesson: Jesus is the light of our lives. He supplies our every need.

Materials: Radish or bean seeds, small jars, porous paper such as paper towels, water and metal foil.

Procedure: Line the jars with paper. Stiff paper such as blotting paper holds the seed in position better than tissue paper or paper towels. Put several seeds around the side of each jar between the glass and the paper. Pour a little water into each jar. Cover the outside of some jars with metal foil. Arrange the covered and uncovered jars so some are in a dark place, others in a shaded area, and others in direct sunlight. As time passes, have the students make observations and inferences regarding what plants need for proper growth.

Principles of growth

Objective: To show that plant stems are designed to grow upward despite the angle at which a seed is planted.

Spiritual lesson: No matter what our situation in life, God wants us to grow closer to Him.

Materials: Small pots or empty milk cartons (preferably with holes for drainage), good soil, and seeds ready to plant. (Large seeds such as beans or corn work best.)

Procedure: Carefully plant seeds in one pot "upside down," "sideways" in another pot, and "right side up" in the third. Two or three of the same kind of seed should be in each pot. Be certain to cover the seeds with approximately the same amount of dirt. Put the containers in a warm place that gets plenty of sunlight and be sure to keep them watered. Avoid too much watering. Soil should never get completely dry, but always soaking wet isn't good.

Results: The roots always grow downward and the stems upward. Appropriate questions and observations made during the course of plant growth allow students to make inferences. That is, to draw conclusions or make deductions based on their observation.

Additional observation: What may be inferred about the Creator who designed plants?

Siphoning for fun

Objective: To make inferences about the forces that cause water to flow "uphill."

Spiritual lesson: Because of God's power, we can do things we may think at first are impossible.

Materials: A clear plastic or rubber tube 15 or

more inches long, and two containers to hold water, such as large plastic or glass jars. Food coloring added to the water will make it more visible.

Procedure: Fill one container with water. Place one end of the tube into the beaker and suck up the water until it nearly fills the tube. The tube may also be filled with water by carefully immersing it into the filled container. Leave one end of the tube in the filled container, and with the other end closed off, arrange the tube so there is an obvious "uphill" and "downhill." The other container should be on a lower level and is used to catch the siphoned water. Watch the water levels change and discuss the water's movement. Be careful to keep the higher end of the tube under water.

Result: Water flows upward from one container and then downward to the other. Students may discuss the forces causing the water to flow "uphill."

Ice-cream-stick boat

Objective: To make inferences regarding the forces causing the boat to move on still water.

Spiritual lesson: The aid of the Holy Spirit moves us forward for Christ.

Materials: Small wooden boat carved from a one-inch piece of ice-cream stick (or simply cut from heavy paper), basin, water, an eyedropper, and soap or oil. Camphor oil, salad oil, or other light oil may work.

Procedure: Cut the boat with a keyhole or v-shaped notch at one end. Fill the basin with water and carefully set the boat on the water. Avoid wetting the upper side of the boat. With the eyedropper, place some oil in the circular part of the keyhole. The oil spreads evenly in all directions and presses against all parts of the hole. Ask why the boat moves forward. Alternatively, softened bar soap may be pressed into the notch before launching.

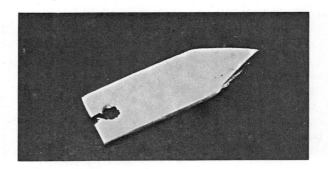

Explanation: The boat moves forward because pressure acts against the front of the hole. Pressure toward the opening of the hole is against the water but not the boat. This difference in pressure causes the boat to move forward.

Cutting ice

Objective: To figure out from observation how the ice was cut.

Spiritual lesson: Asking Jesus to cut away sin will not help us if we go back to it again.

Materials: Ice, thin wire, and weights to be attached to wire. To get a block of ice large enough to use, you may need to freeze it.

Procedure: Tie the weights to the ends of the wire. Drape the wire over the middle of the ice with the two weights on either side. Let the weights pull the wire through the ice.

Increased pressure causes the ice to melt at a temperature below 32°F. As the wire passes through the ice it again freezes above the wire. Thus the ice will be in one piece after the wire has cut through it.

Explanation: Heat is not the only thing that causes ice to melt. Pressure does too. Here the pressure or pushing down of the wire melts the ice, but when the wire moves down and the extra pressure is gone, the water freezes again.

Break a pencil with water

Objective: Infer why objects placed in water appear broken.

Spiritual lesson: If life seems bent or broken to you, go to God and His word for instructions for rearranging it.

Materials: Glass tumbler, water and a pencil.

Procedure: Fill the tumbler with water. Place the pencil in the water so that part of it is beneath the water. Look at it from a distance of several feet and from several different locations. Observe how the pencil seems to be broken at the surface of the water. Notice also that the part beneath the water appears enlarged.

Results: Light rays bend as they enter or leave the water. This is called refraction. This makes the pencil appear broken at the surface of the water. What you are looking at is not straight ahead of your line of sight as it seems. You see where the rays leave the water and the glass. The curvature of the water acts like a magnifying lens. This causes enlargement.

Questions like "Is the pencil really broken?" and "If not, why does it look like it is?" will lead students in their thinking. The explanation, however, isn't obvious, so you will probably need to tell them unless they already know about light bending.

Note: Refraction also causes water to look shallower. Take two tumblers and place a coin in each one. Then fill one with water, and compare the appearances of the coins looking down through the tops of the tumblers.

You may also want to place a coin in a cereal bowl and move back to where it is barely hidden by the side of the bowl. Ask someone to pour water into the bowl while you watch the coin reappear.

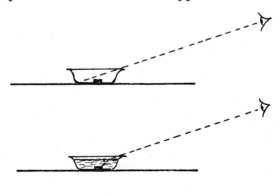

Inferring / 96

Density of water

Objective: Students should be able to: (1) demonstrate that salt water has greater buoyancy than fresh water, (2) explain why it is easier to float in the sea than it is to float in fresh water.

Spiritual lesson: Hebrews 10:22. Because Jesus is our Representative in heaven we can come near in "full assurance of faith, our hearts sprinkled clean from an evil conscience and our bodies washed with pure water."

Materials: Pencil stubs 3 to 4 inches long, a small cup, salt and a graduated cylinder or other narrow cylindrical container such as a large test tube to hold floating pencils in a vertical position. A fruit jar will work if you tape paper clips to the bottom end of the pencil as illustrated.

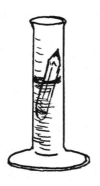 

Procedure: (1) Fill the container nearly full with water. (2) Drop the pencil in it with the eraser end downward. (3) Tap to free the pencil from the edge of the container and observe the location of the water line on the pencil. (4) Pour the water into a paper cup and add one teaspoon of salt. Stir until dissolved. (5) Pour the salt water back into the container and float the pencil as previously described and again observe the location of the water line on the pencil. (6) Repeat steps four and five until no more salt will dissolve. A scale may be scratched on the pencil stub to facilitate the measurements. Ask students to make inferences resulting from their observations.

Explanation: As the salt concentration increases, the pencil stub will need to displace less liquid to equal its weight. Hence, the stub floats at a higher level.

Note: The pencil in this experiment is used as an instrument called a hydrometer. One use of hydrometers is to measure the density of milk. Milk with more cream is less dense making the hydrometer float with less above the surface.

Which popcorn is best?

Objective: To make inferences relating the kernel size and resulting volume of the popped corn.

Spiritual lesson: The Lord expects a person to use his talents in proportion to the way they have been given.

Materials: Popcorn, a balance capable of weighing small objects, and a means of popping corn. A hot air popper is recommended.

Procedure: Give each student twenty kernels of corn. Then ask them to follow these instructions: (1) Pick out the five largest and five smallest kernels. (2) Weigh all ten. (3) Pop them without adding anything. Weigh all ten again. (4) Note the difference in weight.

At home or in a school without a sensitive balance, a larger amount of popcorn may be used weighing before and after on a postal scales.

Inferring: Appropriate questions such as the following will help make inferences. "What causes the corn to pop when heated?."

Explanation: Kernels require moisture inside to pop. Steam pressure causes their explosion.

Additional investigation: Compare various characteristics of corn kernels. Get sweet corn (as seeds), animal feed corn (from a feed store), and several varieties of popcorn.

What dissolves in water?

Objective: To make inferences about the nature of things that dissolve in water.

Spiritual lesson: The Holy Spirit comes to each of us to melt the sin from our hearts, but He can do nothing unless we are willing.

Materials: Four glasses, salt, sugar, flour, sand and water.

Procedure: Put one tablespoon of each substance to be tested into a separate container. Fill each with water and stir. Observe which substances dissolve and which do not.

Results: Flour and sand do not dissolve, but the salt and sugar do.

Explanation: Water will dissolve some substances but will not disolve others. The molecules of the substances it dissolves sometimes break into two parts called ions.
Students may be aware of the differences between oil-based and water-based paints. Water will not clean oil paint from a brush, but will clean a brush used in a water-base paint and vice versa.

For further investigation: Other "solutes" and "solvents" may be tested.

Water content in food

Objective: To infer purposes of the skin on fruits and vegetables.

Spiritual lessons: (1) The Creator made a way to keep food fresh until we are ready to eat it. (2) The way God has shown us to live gives protection from evil.

Materials: Balance (scales), long needle, heavy thread and several samples of fresh fruits.

Procedure: (1) Take each kind of fruit; slice

about half and leave the rest unpeeled.

(2) Use the needle to string the fruit along lengths of thread. Do not mix peeled and unpeeled or different kinds of fruit on the same string.

(3) Mark each string of fruit for later identification and weigh it carefully.

(4) Hang all the fruit in a sunny, well-ventilated location.

(5) Weigh the strings three times a week.

(6) Make a graph showing weight on the vertical scale and number of days on the horizontal scale. Infer purposes of the fruit's skin from this experiment and think of other possible purposes.

The green bean

Objective:　To help students realize the relationship between our sight and our enjoyment of food.

Spiritual lesson:　Man looks at the outside appearance and judges, but God looks at the heart.

Materials:　One package of frozen green beans, one-half cup of water, one teaspoon of baking soda, one pot, and a heat source for cooking.

Procedure:　Put the beans, the water and the baking soda in the cooking pot and bring it to a boil. Note how the baking soda has turned the color of the beans to a delicious-looking bright green.　Have the students taste the beans.

Results: The beans will be a beautiful bright green, but they will taste terrible. Fried eggs colored green, blue mashed potatoes and other similar strange colored foods may be used to help students make inferences regarding food preferences.

Substances that burn

Objective: To make inferences about burning substances.

Spiritual lesson: With the Holy Spirit in our lives we will become as the materials that don't burn. Things around us may burst into flame but we will be under control.

Materials: String, paper, copper wire, cloth, wood, plastic, and some aluminum foil.

Procedure: With forceps or other holders (tweezers), attempt to burn each of the materials available and record any changes in the material. Ask the students what they can infer about those that burn.

Results: The materials produced from living things are more likely to burn.

Note: Students may make incorrect inferences such as that aluminum and iron will not burn, but that is to be expected. Aluminum, magnesium and even steel wool will burn under the right conditions. For example, steel wool when heated red hot and placed in a pure oxygen atmosphere burns dramatically.

Oxygen can be obtained for demonstration purposes by reacting peroxide with manganese dioxide from a discarded dry cell.   Fresh dry yeast may be used to release oxygen rather than using manganese dioxide.

Where there's smoke there's fire

Objective: To make inferences about the nature of fire.

Spiritual lesson: Even if Satan blows out the light of truth in a part of the world, God can rekindle it.

Materials: A candle and some matches.

Procedure: Light a candle and allow it to burn until a pool of wax is visible. Blow out the flame. Re-light the candle by holding a lighted match in the smoke trail but not touching the wick.

Results: The candle will again ignite without the flame coming into direct contact with the wick. Under good conditions the candle can be lit from as far as an inch away.   Students should notice that smoke usually indicates incomplete burning and that the flame is produced mostly from the burning of the wax rather than the wick.

Predicting

Floating boats

Objective: To discover what factors determine the payload a boat can carry.

Spiritual lesson: The Lord knows us and He will not allow us to be tempted beyond what we are able to endure, if we ask for His help.   See 1 Cor. 10:13.

Materials: Aluminum foil and/or oil-based modeling clay, water, paper clips or other small weights.

Procedure: Have the children make boats from the given material.   Tell them to design their boats as they like as long as they will float.   Have students describe the features that make boats float.   Then ask them to experiment to find a design to carry the maximum load.

Based on experience, ask each student or team of students to predict the paper-clip capacity of the other students' boats or of another boat they design. Then test the predictions.

You will probably want to weigh the clay portions carefully so all will be the same.

Learning from spools

Objective: To develop prediction skill by observing spools turned in simulation of pulley systems.

Spiritual lesson: Our words and actions often cause other people to react. It is important to set the best example, to turn in the right direction.

Materials: Several small-headed nails, scrap boards, empty thread spools of various sizes, and rubber bands.

Procedure: Mount the spools on the scrap board so they turn easily. Mark one side of the visible end of each spool to make it easy to watch. Number or color the mounted spools so they may be easily referred to. Connect the spools with rubber bands, some with one twist and others without a twist. Ask, after adding each band, for students to predict what will happen if a given spool is turned.

Weather check

Objective: To understand the meaning of accuracy in weather prediction.

Spiritual lesson: In nature, God has given us many warning signs to tell us when a storm is on the way or to inform us that good weather is ahead. The Bible also uses world conditions as warning signs. (See Matthew 24.)

Materials: A record book.

Procedure: Ask your students to do the following: From newspapers or evening TV forecasts, make a log of predictions for 10 days. The days do not need to be consecutive (all in a row without a break). Also record actual weather conditions. Then figure what fraction of days the predictions were correct. You might limit your data to cloud cover, precipitation and/or high temperature within one degree Fahrenheit or Celsius (depending on which you use for recording). The fractions may be changed to percent accuracy.

Yeast activity

Objective: To help students see why yeast is used in bread.

Spiritual lesson: Yeast grows only under certain conditions. In the same way we must remember that just going to church or just being nice is not going to guarantee us heaven. We need the love of Jesus and the Holy Spirit in our lives.

Materials: Four teaspoonfuls of dry yeast, four clear glasses, a tablespoonful of sugar, and four cups of warm water.

Procedure: Before the children start the experiment, talk about the fact that people use yeast in bread to make it rise. Tell them what you are about to do and ask them to predict what will happen to each of the mixtures in the glasses. Place one teaspoon of dry yeast in each of the four glasses.

One of the glasses should contain only yeast, the second should have one tablespoon of sugar added to the yeast, the third should have one cup of warm water added to the yeast, and the fourth should have one tablespoon of sugar and one cup of warm water added to the yeast. As they follow the procedures, have them record what happens to the yeast in each situation. When the yeast in the last glass begins to grow, have them predict how long it will take the yeast to rise to the top of the glass. Encourage them to explain why the results in the fourth glass differed from the others.

Making colors

Objective: Students should learn to make the colors they want from the the primary colors and also learn predicting skills.

Spiritual lesson: God in His infinite wisdom has created a wide variety of colors for our pleasure.

Materials: Red, blue, and yellow food colorings diluted in water.

Procedure: Mix red and blue and observe. Do the same for blue and yellow, and for yellow and red. The red and blue will make purple. The blue and yellow make green, and yellow and red make orange. Students will want to make other colors. If students are required to match colors in sample bottles, they will need to guess and adjust the amounts. They could count drops from a medicine dropper or use a hypodermic syringe (without the needle).

Results: If careful records are kept, the colors produced by certain formulas may be accurately predicted.

Ripening of bananas

Objective: To develop skills in prediction.

Spiritual lesson: Just as the fruit needs certain conditions to become ripe and useful, so we need the condition of God's Word and continued commitment for the development of "ripe" characters.

Materials: Several green bananas.

Procedure: Children are to make two lists. The first one should describe the properties of green bananas and the second should describe the properties of ripe bananas. Ask them to guess what conditions might affect the ripening process such as light, temperature, the amount of air surrounding the fruit, and the fruit nearby that is already ripe. Place several green bananas in different places in the room (in the closet, on the windowsill, in a plastic bag with ripe bananas, etc.). Observe whether the bananas ripen faster in the light or in darkness, and whether the lack of air surrounding the fruit will cause a fruit to ripen more easily.

Putting bananas in the refrigerator will show that skin color isn't always a good indication of ripeness. We would define riper as sweeter and softer. Sugar is formed in fruit as complex carbohydrate molecules break up into smaller ones. We call this process ripening.

For fun: Puncture a banana at several black spots with a long pin. Move the pin from side to side to slice the banana without slicing the skin. Then you could predict that your friend, on peeling the banana, will find it already sliced.

Why we wash our hands

Objective: To show children why it is important to wash their hands before handling food; and to be able to predict the condition of contaminated food.

Spiritual lesson: At first, sin cannot be detected just as the potatoes look alike, but soon, if left to grow, sin takes over like the growth on the potato peeled with unwashed hands.

Materials: Two unpeeled potatoes, a knife, and two sterilized glass jars.

Procedure: Have two children volunteer to help with the experiment. Send one of them to the washroom to wash his or her hands as clean as possible. Leave the second child with his hands unwashed. Have each child peel a potato and place it in a sterile jar. Label the jars with the students' names and write on the front "Hands washed" or "Hands unwashed" as the case may be. Place the jars on the science table and observe from day to day to note changes.

Note: See the comment about germs and soap for the experiment, "Germs don't like soap."

Filtering

Objective: To learn about capillary action by seeing how suspended matter is filtered out of water passing through a cloth wick, and to hypothesize about the results of passing dirty water through a wick by capillary action.

Spiritual lesson: Just as clear water is separated from the muddy water, so the Lord will separate the sin from our lives if we want Him to.

Materials: Three bowls, water, flannel or wool strips braided or twisted together to form a wick, and loose-weave cloth.

Procedure: Ask students to stir some soil into a bowl of water. Some of the soil will remain suspended and will discolor the water. Pour the mixture through a loose-weave cotton cloth, asking students to observe what happens.

Ask the students to place an empty bowl on top of a box or step. Place one end of a wet length of wick in the bowl and drape the other end over the side so that it hangs down into a second bowl.

Ask the students to guess what will happen when the strained water is poured into the top bowl. Then pour it in and watch.

Results: Drops of clear water will fall from the free end of the wick. Capillary action draws the water from the top bowl leaving the suspended matter behind. CAUTION students that the water is still not pure for drinking.

Barometer

Objective: To help children learn the purpose of a barometer and how it works.

Spiritual lesson: Our faith may fluctuate, but Christ never changes.

Materials: Wide mouth jar, balloon, two rubber bands, drinking straw, tape, scissors, and construction paper. (Thin balloon rubber may leak air faster than thicker rubber and would be less satisfactory. You could try Saran Wrap® or plastic from a plastic bag, although the latter may not seal as well to the jar.)

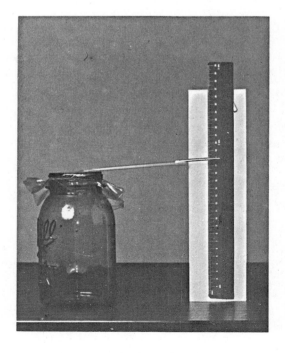

Predicting / 114

Procedure: Cut a piece of the balloon large enough to fit over the mouth of the jar, stretch it tightly across the jar's mouth making sure it seals well. Hold it in place with two rubber bands or a jar ring. Tape one end of the straw to the center of the balloon. Fold the construction paper into a triangular tube and tape it together. Attaching a ruler is optional. Put the tube next to the pointed end of the straw (Do not let them touch.) Make a pencil line on the tube where the pointer points and write the weather condition next to that line.

Check once or twice a day. Each time the pointer moves, draw a line and write down the weather condition. After marking some sunny and some stormy results, you can predict the weather.

A barometer measures air pressure. When the air outside the jar pushes harder, the rubber moves down and the pointer goes up indicating that the weather is expected to be fair. With reduced atmospheric pressure, the pointer goes down to show that a storm may be approaching. The barometer's value as a predicting instrument lies in the fact that the air pressure usually changes before a change is noticed in the weather.

A commercially made barometer will give better results for predicting weather. Also, the fruit-jar barometer will be a little better indicator if kept at the same temperature because temperature as well as pressure affect it.

Discuss: If the air pushes in on us all the time (at more than 14 pounds per square inch), why don't we we feel it? **Answer:** Pressure inside pushes out to balance the pressure from the air. We *do* feel it when the pressure inside our ears hasn't had opportunity to balance when a change occurs rapidly.

Covering a lighted candle

Objective: To learn that air is needed for burning.

Spiritual lesson: When we cover our light, it eventually goes out. (Matt. 5:14-16; 25:1-13; Isa. 60:1-3).

Materials: A candle, a bowl, matches, and two or three jars of different sizes. Heat may break jars. You could try birthday candles or larger jars, if this is a problem. (Hot glass can also burn fingers.)

Procedure: Stand a candle in a shallow bowl or dish and light it. Invert the smallest jar (turn it upside down) over the candle and time the interval it takes until the candle goes out. Repeat, using larger jars, asking students to predict how long the flame will last.

Note: The flame uses oxygen from the air and makes carbon dioxide gas. When most of the oxygen is used up, the fire goes out.

Predicting angles

Objective: To show that the direction of light reflected from a mirror is like the angle at which a ball bounces off of a flat object, and that one can be predicted in the same way the other can.

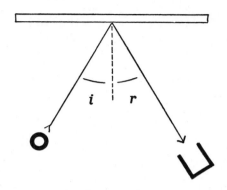

Spiritual lesson: God has given us simple things to help us understand the complicated ones. Parables help us understand spiritual truths.

Materials: A good flat board or wall, a mirror, a rubber ball or a table-tennis ball, and a box for a goal.

Procedure: This activity involves figuring out how to get a ball to roll into a box after being bounced off of a wall or other vertical flat surface. After the students have practiced a little, mount a mirror on the board or wall. Let the students discover how to predict the way to roll the ball from looking into the mirror. Ask one student to look into the mirror and predict where to position the box in order for the ball to roll into it. Have the students change angles, or get closer or farther from the mirror and try again.

Students will learn that the *angle of incidence* equals the *angle of reflection.*

Introducing inertia

Objective: To learn that moving things have a tendency to keep moving in the same direction unless something pulls on them or stops them, and to learn predicting skills.

Spiritual lesson: Disregarding God's laws of nature brings disaster.

Materials: Three or four books, and a string with a soft ball attached.

Procedure: Place the books on a person's head. Have him or her walk quickly and then stop suddenly. Repeat this several times, asking him to predict what will happen.

Swing the ball in a horizontal, circular path while holding on to the string. Ask the students to predict what will happen when the string is released.

The ball will no longer move in a circular path but in a straight line tangent to its original circular path. Illustrate what has happened on the chalkboard.

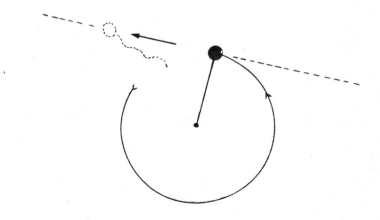

Effects of inertia

Objective: To better understand what inertia is and to be able to predict its effects.

Spiritual lesson: Jesus (the card) is our foundation.   When we allow Him to be taken away from us, we (like the coin) fall into the pit of sin (the tumbler).

Materials: A shoe box with an end removed and a ball.   Also a glass tumbler (drinking glass), a small size index card, and a coin.

Procedure: Put the shoe box upside down on a table with the ball in it.   Move the box, open end forward, along a table and then stop the box suddenly after it has traveled 1/3 of the distance across the table.   Observe what happens to the ball.   Explain the above situation to the children and ask that they predict what will happen in the following situation, reminding them that things in motion tend to stay in motion and things at rest tend to stay at rest.   Place the index card over the mouth of the glass.   Put the coin on top of the card, positioning the coin so that it is at the center of the glass.
After the children have predicted what might happen, snap the card from under the coin with your finger.

Result: In the first experiment the inertia of the ball will make it continue to travel in a straight line on the table top.   In the second experiment, the coin will stay at rest for an instant when the card is moved quickly.   Then, as inertia is overcome, the coin drops.

Note: Seat belts could be discussed in connection with this activity.